101 PRESIDENT JOKES

by Melvin Berger
Illustrated by H.L. Schwadron

SCHOLASTIC INC.
New York Toronto London Auckland Sydney

For Nancy and Mitch
my favorite joke mavens

ISBN 0-590-43166-8

12 11 10 9 8 7   2 3 4 5/9

Printed in the U.S.A.   01

First Scholastic printing, January 1990

GEORGE WASHINGTON
1st President — 1789–1797

Young George Washington
probably did not chop down his
father's cherry tree. And he
probably did not admit it by saying,
"I cannot tell a lie."

But many people repeat that
story because it shows
Washington's honesty.

Little Suzy once asked her
mother, "Do people who never tell
lies go to heaven?"

"Yes," her mother answered.
"They are the only ones."

"Gosh, I bet it's lonesome up
there with just God and George
Washington."

Everyone learns about George Washington in school. A teacher once asked her class, "Was Washington a great general or a great admiral?"

Willy replied, "A great general."

"How do you know?" the teacher asked.

"I saw a picture of Washington crossing the Delaware," said Willy. "And no admiral would stand up in such a small boat!"

In 1787 Washington led the convention that wrote the U.S. Constitution. He spoke little during this historic meeting.

Then someone suggested that the Constitution set a limit of 5,000 men in the army.

Washington could be quiet no longer. "If that is so," he said, "let the Constitution also say that no foreign army should ever invade our country with more than 3,000 troops."

THOMAS JEFFERSON
3rd President — 1801–1809

Thomas Jefferson was a great believer in the people. He wanted them to watch out for lies that were passed off as the truth.

"Advertisements contain the only truth to be relied on in a newspaper," he warned.

Also, "The man who reads nothing at all is better educated than the man who reads nothing but newspapers."

JAMES MADISON
4th President — 1809–1817

President James Madison was the shortest of all the Presidents. He stood at just over five feet tall. One day a visitor came to see him for the first time. The President's secretary said, "The President can't be seen."

"My God!" the visitor exclaimed, "Is he that short?"

JOHN QUINCY ADAMS
6th President — 1825–1829

President John Quincy Adams, the eldest son of the second President, John Adams (1797–1801), was a man of fixed habits. Every morning he did the same things: Rise at five. Start the fire. Read the Bible. And then go for either a walk or a swim.

While he was swimming in the Potomac one day, someone stole his clothes. A little later, a young boy walked by. He was surprised to see a short, fat, naked man come out of the water. He was even more surprised when the man asked him to run to the White House and ask Mrs. Adams to send a suit of clothes for the President!

ANDREW JACKSON
7th President — 1829–1837

President Andrew Jackson was born in the backwoods of South Carolina. He had little education and always kept his rough frontier ways. One day a Senator brought an elegant English lady to meet President Jackson. Before showing her in, the Senator said to Jackson, "Put on your very best manners."

President Jackson was furious. "Senator," he shouted, "I never heard of a fellow getting ahead by minding someone else's manners."

President Jackson used to tell
about a Frenchman who boasted
that King Louis had spoken to him.

"What did the king say to you?"
someone asked.

"He said, 'Get out of my way!'"

MARTIN VAN BUREN
8th President — 1837–1841

   John Van Buren, son of President
Martin Van Buren, made up the
famous line about cheating at an
election: "Vote early — and vote
often."

President Van Buren liked to give speeches that pleased people on both sides of an issue. In one case, people in the North wanted a tax on imported wool. People in the South wanted no tax. The President took an hour to explain his position.

When he was through, one listener turned to another and said, "That was a good speech."

"Yes, it was very good," his friend agreed.

Then he paused and asked, "But is the President for or against the wool tax?"

15

JOHN TYLER
10th President — 1841–1845

President John Tyler was a very good politician. He knew when to speak and when to keep quiet. He also knew how to say exactly the right thing.

One time a reporter asked him, "Do you want Texas to become part of the United States?"

Tyler answered, "Half of my friends are for it. Half are against it. And I stand with my friends!"

MILLARD FILLMORE
13th President — 1850–1853

When President Zachary Taylor died on July 8, 1850, Vice-President Millard Fillmore became President.

On taking office, President Fillmore decided he should have a fancy carriage. He went with his assistant, Edward Moran, to look at a carriage. It was being sold by someone who was leaving Washington.

"It's very fine," said Fillmore. "But should a President be seen in a secondhand carriage?"

"Remember, sir," Moran reminded him, "that you're a secondhand President."

FRANKLIN PIERCE
14th President — 1853–1857

When Franklin Pierce was running for President, his opponents made fun of his record during the Mexican War. They printed a book called *The Military Service of Franklin Pierce*. The book was very odd. It was only one inch tall and a half inch wide!

After Franklin Pierce was elected President, several reporters went to his hometown of Hillsboro, New Hampshire. They asked a local shopkeeper about President Pierce. "We all know Franklin," he said. "And we think he's a good man. But if you spread him out over the whole country, I'm afraid he'll be awful thin in spots."

ABRAHAM LINCOLN
16th President — 1861–1865

Abraham Lincoln was giving a campaign speech before a very unfriendly crowd. At the end, someone yelled out, "I wouldn't vote for you if you were St. Peter himself!"

"My friend," replied Lincoln, "if I were St. Peter, you could not possibly vote for me. You would not be in my district!"

Abraham Lincoln was a lawyer before he became President. Next to his desk, he kept his tall stovepipe hat. As he worked, he put his papers into the hat.

When the hat got full, he dumped the papers onto the floor. On top of the pile, he left a note: "If you can't find it anywhere else, look here."

President Lincoln knew that people don't always see their own faults. He told about a farmer he knew. The farmer said, "I'm not greedy. All I want is the land next to mine."

Ward Lamon, a fellow lawyer, ripped the back of his pants just before going to court with Lincoln. Another lawyer passed around a paper, asking for contributions to buy Lamon a new pair of pants. When the paper came around to Lincoln, he wrote, "I can contribute nothing to the end in view."

Certain people in Lincoln's time thought that "Honest Abe" sometimes lied. They said he was two-faced. To one critic, Lincoln said, "If I had another face, do you think I would use this one?"

Lincoln was very tall, as thin as a rail, and not at all good-looking. One day a man said to him, "I hear you're a self-made man."

"So they say," Lincoln replied.

The man looked him over from head to toe. "Well, you didn't do a very good job, did you," he snickered.

Young Abe Lincoln fought in the Black Hawk War. His troop was led by a very short captain. One day the captain shouted at the six-foot, four-inch Lincoln. "Stand up tall!"

Just before straightening up, Lincoln leaned over and said, "Farewell, Captain. I fear I shall never see you again."

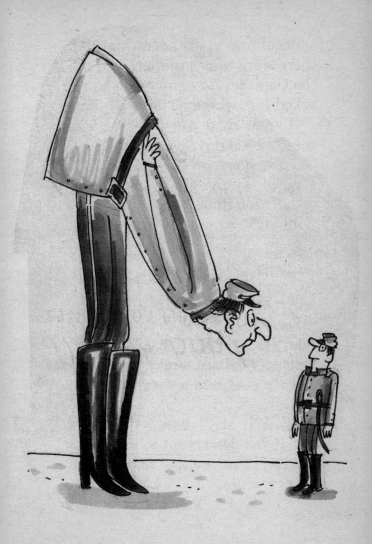

According to President Lincoln, there were over a million men in the Confederate Army. A listener asked him where he got that figure.

"I know there are 400,000 men in the Union Army," said Lincoln. "And whenever we lose a battle, the general says he was outnumbered 3 to 1. Three times 400,000 is over a million."

For a long while during the Civil War, General McClellan did not fight any battles. Finally, President Lincoln sent him a note:

My dear McClellan,
    If you don't want to use the Army, I should like to borrow it for a while.

                Yours respectfully,
                A.L.

During the Civil War, many newspapers had long articles telling President Lincoln how to win the war. By way of reply, he told about a man riding horseback on a dark night. The man lost his way during a terrible storm. Each crash of thunder made the ground shake. But every flash of lightning helped him to see where he was going.

After one very loud clap of thunder, he fell to his knees and prayed. "Dear Lord," he said, "if it's all the same to you, could you please give a little more light and a little less sound?"

General George B. McClellan was always telling Abraham Lincoln how to run the country. A friend asked Lincoln, "What are you going to do about it?"

"Nothing, for now," said Lincoln.

But it did remind him of a story: "A cowboy was riding a horse. All of a sudden, the horse kicked up and stuck his leg through the stirrup. The cowboy looked down and said, 'If you're getting on, I'm getting off.'"

Some of Lincoln's advisers told him to issue a proclamation saying that all the slaves were free. Lincoln insisted that *saying* they were free would not *make* them free.

To explain, he asked, "If you call a sheep's tail a leg, how many legs does a sheep have?"

"Five," the advisers agreed.

"No. A sheep only has four legs," said Lincoln. "Calling a tail a leg doesn't make it so."

Lincoln believed that people should not put on airs or think too highly of themselves.

"What kills a skunk is the publicity it gives itself," he said.

Lincoln jokes continue, right on to the present. Just the other day a mother boasted, "My son Johnny is smarter than Lincoln. Lincoln didn't give the Gettysburg Address until he was fifty. Johnny gave it when he was ten!"

ANDREW JOHNSON
17th President — 1865–1869

President Andrew Johnson had many enemies in government. When he was trying to explain his position to some Senators, he asked, "Did you hear my last speech?"

A voice answered, "I hope so!"

ULYSSES S. GRANT
18th President — 1869–1877

President Ulysses S. Grant
boasted that he knew only two
tunes. "One of them is 'Yankee
Doodle.' The other isn't."

CHESTER A. ARTHUR
21st President — 1881–1885

This story may or may not be true, but it has been said that President Chester Arthur went on a tour of a prison. At the end, he was asked to say a few words.

"My fellow citizens. . . ," he began. But he stopped because in those days people lost their citizenship while in prison.

"My fellow convicts. . . ," he tried next. No, that didn't sound right either.

Finally he found an opening. "Well, anyhow, I'm glad to see so many of you here."

GROVER CLEVELAND
22nd President — 1885–1889
24th President — 1893–1897

President Grover Cleveland went
on a fishing trip with two friends.
Before they left, they agreed that
whoever caught the first fish would
treat the others to dinner.

Later, President Cleveland
complained that his friends were
not fair. "They both had bites," he
explained, "but did not pull up the
fish."

"Then I suppose you had to buy
dinner for everyone," said a
listener.

"No," President Cleveland
answered with a smile. "I didn't
have any bait on my hook!"

President Cleveland was always fighting with the Senate. But he got along very well with the House of Representatives.

One night when he was fast asleep, Mrs. Cleveland shook him awake. "There are thieves in the house," she whispered.

"No, my dear," the President answered. "Thieves in the Senate, maybe. But not in the House."

Many Americans felt that President Cleveland did not know how bad things were during the Depression of 1893. This joke made the rounds at the time:

A man without any money and no job came to the White House. He got down on his knees and started chewing the grass.

"What are you doing?" the President asked.

"I'm hungry and I have nothing else to eat," the man replied.

President Cleveland thought for a moment. "Well, then you should go to the backyard. The grass is taller there."

WILLIAM McKINLEY
25th President — 1897–1901

A story is told about the time President William McKinley was showing a tourist around Washington, D.C. The President pointed out the place where George Washington supposedly threw a dollar across the Potomac River.

"So what?" exclaimed the tourist. "A dollar went much farther in those days."

The first football game that President McKinley ever saw was between Princeton and Yale. Later he said he was disappointed. "It was no game at all. They got into a scrap and kept fighting all the time they should have been playing ball."

THEODORE ROOSEVELT
26th President — 1901–1909

President Theodore Roosevelt was always seeking adventure and excitement. A visitor once said that she hoped that the President would not get the country into a war. The President jumped up, saying "What? Have a war with me cooped up here in the White House? Never!"

WILLIAM H. TAFT
27th President — 1909–1913

William Howard Taft was a Republican. At the end of a campaign speech, he asked everyone to vote for him. One man stood up. "Not me!" he declared.

"Why not?" Taft asked.

"Because my father and grandfather were both Democrats. And I'm a Democrat, too."

"That's not a good reason," Taft pointed out. "What if you were all horse thieves?"

"Well, then I guess we'd all be Republicans," said the man.

At 330 pounds, William Howard Taft weighed more than any other President. Before being elected President, Taft was the governor-general of the Philippines. He sent his reports to Elihu Root, Secretary of War. At the end of one report, Taft wrote, "Took a long horseback ride today. Feel fine."

Root wired back, "How's the horse?"

Here's another story about President Taft's great size: The President was swimming, off the North Carolina coast. A boy who lived nearby was about to jump into the water, but he turned away. "I can't go in. The President is using the ocean," he explained.

President Taft was known as the
most polite man in Washington. On
a train, he would get up and give
his seat to three women!

WOODROW WILSON
28th President — 1913–1921

Before becoming President, Woodrow Wilson was governor of New Jersey. While Wilson was serving as governor, a New Jersey Senator died. Within a few hours, a politician called the governor and said, "I'd like to take the Senator's place."

Governor Wilson was shocked that the politician had called so soon after the Senator's death. But Wilson got even. He told the caller, "It's all right with me — if the undertaker doesn't mind."

President Wilson had a favorite limerick:

For beauty I am no star
There are many more handsome by
   far,
But my face, I don't mind it,
Because I am behind it.
It's the people in front that I jar.

WARREN G. HARDING
29th President — 1921–1923

   The famous lawyer Clarence
Darrow did not like President
Warren Harding. As Darrow put it,
"When I was a boy, I was told that
anyone could be President. Now I'm
beginning to believe it."

CALVIN COOLIDGE
30th President — 1923–1929

President Calvin Coolidge was a man of very few words. One Sunday he went to church. But his wife, Grace, stayed home. When he returned, she asked, "Was the sermon good?"

"Yup," was Coolidge's brief reply.

"What was it about?" Grace asked.

"Sin."

"And what did the minister say?"

"He's against it."

President Coolidge once asked
some of his old friends from
Vermont to dine with him at the
White House. Worried that their
country table manners were not
good enough for a formal dinner,
the guests decided to watch
President Coolidge and do exactly
what he did.

Everything went very well until
it was time for coffee. They noticed
that he poured his coffee into the
saucer. They did the same.

Then the President added sugar
and milk to the coffee. Again, they
imitated him.

Finally Coolidge did something
that stopped them cold. He leaned
over and put the saucer on the floor
for the cat!

One time Coolidge was at the barbershop in his hometown of Plymouth, Vermont. While Coolidge's hair was being cut, the town doctor was waiting his turn.

After several minutes, the doctor asked Coolidge, "Did you take those pills I gave you?"

Coolidge paused before he answered. "Nope."

Some more time passed. Then the doctor spoke again. "Do you feel better?"

Several minutes went by. "Yup," Coolidge finally said.

At last Coolidge's haircut was finished. He started to leave — but without paying the barber.

"You forgot to pay me," the barber reminded him.

"I'm sorry," Coolidge apologized. "I was so busy gossiping with the doctor that it slipped my mind."

Because he was a man of so few words, people called President Coolidge "Silent Cal." But he said he didn't mind. "I've been able to make enough noise to get what I want."

Someone asked Coolidge why he spoke so little. He said, "If you don't say anything, you won't be asked to repeat it."

The most famous Silent Cal story came from a White House dinner:

A woman came over to President Coolidge and said, "I bet someone that I could get you to say three words."

"You lose," was his answer.

Someone bet comedian Will Rogers that he couldn't get the stern-faced Coolidge to laugh. When Rogers was introduced to the President at the White House, the comedian leaned forward and said, "Excuse me, I didn't get the name."

President Coolidge smiled — and Rogers won the bet.

President Coolidge asked a famous minister to eat at the White House before giving his sermon. The minister came, but refused all the food. He said that he could think better on an empty stomach.

President Coolidge and his wife then went to hear the sermon. The President didn't think it was very good. At the end, he turned to Mrs. Coolidge and said, "He might as well have eaten."

Clarence Darrow paid Coolidge a funny sort of compliment. He said, "Coolidge is the greatest man who ever came out of Plymouth, Vermont."

At the beginning of the 1929 Presidential campaign, President Coolidge was asked whether he planned to run again. "I do not choose to run," he said.

One reporter kept after him. "Don't you want to be President again, Mr. Coolidge?" he asked.

"No," replied Coolidge dryly. "There's no chance for advancement."

HERBERT HOOVER
31st President — 1929–1933

In 1932, when Herbert Hoover was President, a phone call cost a nickel. One day President Hoover was out walking with Andrew Mellon, his Secretary of the Treasury. The President suddenly stopped and said, "I just remembered that I have to call a friend, and I have no money. Can you lend me a nickel?"

Mellon reached into his pocket. "Here's a dime. Call all of your friends," was his laughing reply.

A young boy asked President Hoover for his autograph. The President agreed.

When he had finished signing his autograph, the boy held out four more pieces of paper. "Could you sign four more times?" he asked.

"Why?" Hoover asked.

"I can get one Babe Ruth autograph for five of yours," the honest youngster answered.

Al Smith ran for President against Hoover in 1928. At one campaign stop, a heckler called out, "Tell us all you know, Al. It won't take long."

The quick-thinking candidate answered, "I'll do even better. I'll tell all that we both know. It won't take any longer."

FRANKLIN D. ROOSEVELT
32nd President — 1933–1945

During the campaign for his third term, President Franklin D. Roosevelt asked a friend, "Which party are you voting for?"

"I know you're a Democrat," his friend replied. "But I'm voting Republican."

"Why?" the President asked.

"When you first ran, I voted Republican. For your second term, I voted Republican again. And I never had it so good. So I'm going to vote Republican once more!"

The British prime minister Winston Churchill was a frequent guest at the White House while Roosevelt was President. At one dinner, the woman seated next to Churchill kept complaining about his policies. By the end of the meal, she was quite furious with him.

"Mr. Churchill," she shouted, "if I was your wife, I'd put poison in your coffee!"

"Madame," Churchill declared, "if you were my wife, I'd drink it!"

HARRY S. TRUMAN
33rd President — 1945–1953

This story is often told about Harry Truman:

As he was stumping the country for votes, he saw a boy playing in front of a house. "Is your mother home?" Truman asked.

"Yes," the boy answered, without looking up.

Truman knocked on the door. But no one answered.

"I thought you said your mother was home," Truman called out to the youngster.

"She is. But we don't live here."

"I'm looking for an adviser with only one arm," said President Truman. "All the advisers I have now say, 'On the one hand. . . , but on the other hand. . . .' I want someone to give me a single, straight answer."

There is an old saying, "To err is human; to forgive, divine." In the 1948 Presidential campaign, the Republicans changed it to "To err is Truman. . . ."

JOHN F. KENNEDY
35th President — 1961–1963

John Kennedy's father was very, very rich. This led to rumors that he was going to give people money to vote for his son. Making a joke of it, John Kennedy said, "I just got a letter from my father. He says, 'Don't buy one more vote than you need. I'm not going to pay for a landslide.'"

While listening to the election returns, Kennedy spoke on the phone with his running mate, Lyndon Johnson. Later Kennedy reported that Johnson told him, "*You're* losing Ohio, but *we're* doing fine in Pennsylvania."

Robert Kennedy was the campaign manager for his brother John. Sometimes Robert addressed the crowd before his brother did. Robert usually got the crowd laughing with the story of two brothers who went fishing. One brother caught all the fish. The other caught none.

The unlucky one finally asked to borrow his brother's fishing pole. But still he didn't get any bites. Finally a fish jumped out of the water and said, "We're waiting for your brother."

One winter day, President Kennedy gave a breakfast speech in Los Angeles. He was greeted by a big round of applause. "I'm grateful for your kind welcome," he said. "As the cow said to the farmer, 'Thank you for a warm hand on a cold morning.'"

President Kennedy had a favorite story about Texas pride. A man from Boston was visiting the Alamo. A native Texan was bragging about the bravery of the men who had fought there.

After listening for a while, the man from Boston asked, "Did you ever hear of Paul Revere?"

"Oh, yes," the Texan answered. "He's the guy who ran for help."

A small boy asked President Kennedy how he became a war hero. "It was easy," the President answered. "The Japanese sank my boat."

Physical fitness was an important goal for President Kennedy. In line with this, he told a story about Arthur Goldberg, his Secretary of Labor:

Goldberg went mountain climbing. But up near the peak, he got separated from all the others.

The Red Cross sent climbers to try to find him. As they roamed over the mountain they shouted, "Goldberg! Goldberg! It's the Red Cross."

Finally a distant voice echoed down the mountain, saying, "I gave at the office!"

Kennedy was only 43 years old when he was elected President. A popular joke of the time told about a father who said to his son, "When Lincoln was your age, he walked 10 miles to school every day."

And the son answered, "So what? When Kennedy was your age, he was already President!"

"There are three real things in life," John F. Kennedy once said, "God, human folly, and laughter. We can't understand the first two, so we'll just have to make the best of the third."

LYNDON B. JOHNSON
36th President — 1963–1969

In his campaign ads, Lyndon B. Johnson said, "If you vote for Goldwater, your taxes will go up."

Johnson won the election and became President.

Some years later, a voter came up to President Johnson and said, "You know, you really told the truth during the campaign. You said if you vote for Goldwater your taxes will go up. I did vote for Goldwater. And my taxes did go up!"

President Johnson bragged about the bravery of the United States Marines. In a speech he told about a Marine officer who told his men that they would be jumping out of a plane flying at 800 feet.

A few of the men looked worried. Finally one came over to the officer. "Please, sir," he began, "could the plane fly at 500 feet?"

"No, I'm afraid not," he answered. "That's too low for the parachutes to open."

The surprised Marine replied, "Oh, you mean we're going to have parachutes?"

President Johnson had a story for every situation. One time he warned Congress that there would be trouble ahead if the budget went too high. He said he was reminded of the teenager who applied for a job on the railroad.

The foreman of the railroad yard said to the young man, "A train is heading east. Another train is heading west on the same track. What would you do?"

"I'd call my brother," the teenager answered.

"Why would you do that?" the foreman asked.

"Because he's never seen a train wreck," was the reply.

The 1964 Presidential campaign was between Lyndon Johnson and Barry Goldwater. During the campaign, Johnson said many nasty things about his opponent. At one point, Goldwater said, "If I didn't know Barry Goldwater, I would have voted against him myself."

President Johnson was given a long, flowery introduction before giving a speech in Michigan. When the President arose to speak, he said, "I wish my parents were here to hear that introduction. My father would have enjoyed it. And my mother would have believed it."

RICHARD M. NIXON
37th President — 1969–1974

President Richard Nixon didn't always get along with Congress. He once said, "Congress makes so many cuts that if they had to vote on the Ten Commandments only eight would pass!"

This story was told about President Nixon:

To bring his message to all the people, he offered to speak at a prison. As soon as word got out, several inmates called on the warden.

"We want to protest," the leader said. "Listening to the President's speech was not part of our sentence."

GERALD R. FORD
38th President — 1974–1977

After a speech he gave in Omaha, President Gerald Ford met a woman who had not been present. She said to him, "I heard you gave a speech tonight."

President Ford modestly answered, "Oh, it was nothing."

To which the woman replied, "Yes, that's what I heard."

One day President Ford decided to try on his old Navy uniform. It was very tight. He said to his wife: "Something funny happens to old uniforms when you keep them in the closet. They start to shrink around the middle."

President Ford used to play football at the University of Michigan. A teammate from those days once introduced Ford with these words: "I played football with Gerry Ford. I was the quarterback. Gerry was the center. This gave me a completely different view of the President of the United States."

President Ford was a good
athlete. Yet he was known for
being very clumsy. Ford, though,
was able to laugh at himself. For
example, he said, "I can ski for
hours on end."

This comment by President Ford will make you stop and think: "If Lincoln were alive today, he'd roll over in his grave."

While he was President, Ford decided to remove the White House swimming pool. He later said, "You don't need a pool in the White House to get in deep water."

JIMMY CARTER
39th President — 1977–1981

President Jimmy Carter complained that the White House reporters sometimes acted like little children. At one news conference he said: "I'm not going to say anything very important tonight. So you can all put your crayons away."

When President Carter smiled, he showed lots of teeth. He liked to say that the income-tax people did not believe that he really spent $600 a year for toothpaste.

A group of Texas farmers asked President Carter for emergency funds because of a bad drought. President Carter had to refuse. But he decided to fly to Texas to explain why.

On the day he arrived in Texas, it was raining very hard. "You asked me for money," he said in his speech to the farmers. "I could not get you the money. So instead I brought you some rain."

RONALD REAGAN
40th President — 1981–1989

Ronald Reagan often said that he wasn't a very good student when he was young. He recalled his teacher telling his mother, "Young Ron is trying — very trying."

President Reagan was invited to give the graduation address at Eureka College, where he had been a student. He started his talk by saying, "The only reason I was asked to come here was to clean out my gym locker!"

One time Reagan quoted Thomas Jefferson, who said that age should not be a barrier to service to the country.

Then Reagan went on, saying, "And when Tom told me that. . . ."

At age 69, Reagan was the oldest man to be elected President. He used to enjoy making jokes about his age. For example, at his 70th birthday party, he said it was really the 31st anniversary of his 39th birthday.

Some people claimed that Reagan had a poor memory. At a press conference, a reporter said to the President, "You said that you would resign if your memory started to go."

Reagan laughed. "I don't remember saying that."

After a speech in Mexico, President Reagan got very little applause. The next speaker, who spoke in Spanish, was cheered loudly. President Reagan joined in — until the American Ambassador whispered to him, "I wouldn't do that if I were you. She just translated your speech."

Many people complained that President Reagan took actions that went over the heads of Congress. His answer was, "So what? Lots of things go over their heads."

At a summit meeting, President Reagan repeated this story: An American told a Russian, "I can walk into the White House. I can slam my hand on the desk. And I can say that I don't like the way Ronald Reagan is running the country."

The Russian replied: "I can do the same thing in my country. I can walk into the Kremlin. I can slam my hand on the desk. And I can say that I don't like the way Ronald Reagan is running the country."

In the farm belt, President Reagan would often tell about a farmer who owned some dry, rocky land. Over the years, though, the farmer worked very hard on the land. In time he turned it into dark, rich soil.

One day the local minister came to visit. The minister admired the land. He said, "It is remarkable what you have accomplished with the Lord's help."

The farmer scratched his head. "Reverend, I wish you could have seen this place when the Lord was doing it alone."

When he was 73, Reagan ran for a second term. A reporter asked if age would be a factor in the campaign. Reagan replied, "I will not make age an issue. I am not going to take advantage of my opponent's youth."

A favorite Reagan yarn: A Texan was visiting a farmer in Maine. The Texan asked, "How big is your farm?"

The farmer answered, "It goes from the road to that clump of trees and across to the creek. Tell me, how big is your farm?"

"Well," said the Texan, "I can get in my car and drive for an hour before I get to the edge of my farm."

"Oh," said the Maine farmer, "I used to have a car like that myself."

GEORGE BUSH
41st President — 1989–

An emigrant from Russia was brought in to see President Bush.

"I guess you left Russia because you wanted more freedom," the President said.

"No, I had plenty of freedom," said the Russian. "I could not complain."

"Then it must be that there were no opportunities in Russia," the President tried next.

"Oh, I had opportunities," the Russian insisted. "I could not complain."

"Was it that you could not find a nice place to live?" asked the President.

"Not at all. I had a beautiful apartment," said the Russian. "I could not complain."

President Bush looked confused.
"If everything was so good in
Russia, why did you come to
America?"

"Aha!" the Russian crowed. "Here
I can complain!"

This old joke was updated when George Bush became President: A man walked into a hotel. "I'd like a room for tonight," he told the clerk.

"I'm sorry, sir, but we have no more rooms," the clerk answered.

"Not even one room?" the man asked.

"No, sir, we're full tonight," said the clerk.

The man thought for a moment. "Tell me, if President Bush came in and asked for a room, would you give him one?"

"I guess if the President of the United States asked for a room, I could find one for him," the clerk replied.

"Well, President Bush is not coming here tonight. So give me the room you'd give him!"